# SUNDAY SOLOS

## FOR ORGAN

*Preludes, Offertories & Postludes*

ISBN 978-1-61780-643-8

**HAL•LEONARD®**
CORPORATION
7777 W. BLUEMOUND RD. P.O. BOX 13819 MILWAUKEE, WI 53213

Visit Hal Leonard Online at
**www.halleonard.com**

# CONTENTS BY CATEGORY

## Preludes

## Offertories

## Postludes

Note: Many of these arrangements are appropriate for more than one category.

# ALPHABETICAL CONTENTS

# Abide with Me

Electronic and Pipe Organs

Upper: Fr. Horn (Fl.) 8'
Lower: Stgs. 8', 4'
Pedal: Soft 16' to Gt.

Drawbar Organs

Upper: 00 0840 000 (00)
Lower: (00) 5533 200 (0)
Pedal: 4 (0) 2 (0) (Spinet 3)

Words by Henry F. Lyte
Music by William H. Monk

* A slight pause between these phrases increases the effectiveness.

* Release when chime expires.

# America, the Beautiful

Electronic and Pipe Organs

Upper:  Full, with 16' and Light Reed(s)
Lower:  Op. Diap. 8', Vln. Diap. 8', Fl. 8'
        (8' Stgs. if needed)
Pedal:  16' and 8' to balance

Drawbar Organs

Upper:  45  7654 432 (00)
Lower:  (00)  8876 543 (0)
Pedal:  7 (0) 5 (0) (Spinet 6)

Words by Katherine Lee Bates
Music by Samuel A. Ward

*Play detached (**not** staccato) except where slurred.

# Come, Thou Almighty King

Electronic and Pipe Organs

Upper: *f* Comb. 16', 8', and 4' no reeds

Lower: *f* Comb. 8' and 4' no reeds (Sw. to Gt.)

Pedal: **16'** and **8'** to balance

Drawbar Organs

Upper: 40 6678 452 (00)

Lower: (00) 8876 543 (0)

Pedal: 6 (0) 4 (0) (Spinet 5)

Traditional
Music by Felice de Giardini

*Dwelling slightly on the melody notes will make them stand out effectively.

# God and God Alone

Electronic Organs
Upper: Strings 8', 4'
Lower: Melodia 8', Reed 8'
Pedal: 8'
Vib./Trem.: On, Fast

Drawbar Organs
Upper:   63 5322 014
Lower:   (00) 7334 011
Pedal:   13
Vib./Trem.: On, Fast

Words and Music by
Phill McHugh

# Holy Ground

**Electronic Organs**
Upper: Flutes (or Tibias) 16', 4'
Lower: Piano
Pedal: 8'
Vib./Trem: On, Fast

**Drawbar Organs**
Upper: 80 0800 000
Lower: (00) Preset Piano or
62 6425 111
Pedal: 34
Vib./Trem: On, Fast

Words and Music by
Geron Davis

With reverence

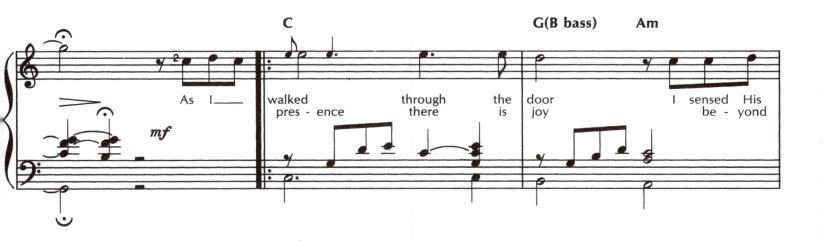

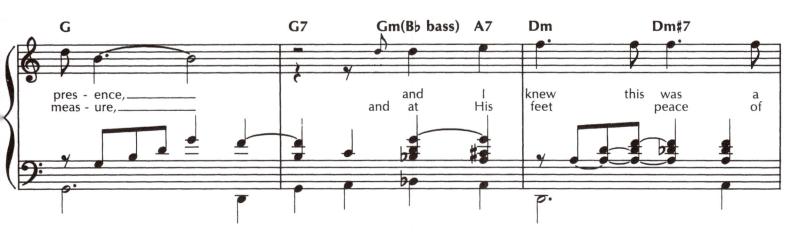

# Just As I Am

*Electronic and Pipe Organs
Upper:  Fr. Horn 8' (Fl. 8')
Lower:  Soft 8' and 4' Stgs.
        (Soft 8' Fl. ad lib)
Pedal:  Soft 16' to Gt.

*Drawbar Organs
Upper:  00  5555 550 (00)
Lower:  (00) 6520 000 (0)
Pedal:  4 (0) 2 (0)  (Spinet 3)

Words by Charlotte Elliott
Music by William B. Bradbury

*Amount of Pedal Tone may be altered to suit room acoustics.
 Use of Vibrato and Reverberation is left to personal preference.

# Lamb of Glory

**Electronic Organs**
Upper: Strings 8', 4', Oboe
Lower: Diapason 8', Flute 8'
Pedals: String Bass
Vib./Trem.: On, Slow

**Drawbar Organs**
Upper: 55 6606 001
Lower: 00 6543 211
Pedals: 46
Vib./Trem.: On, Slow

Words and Music by Greg Nelson
and Phill McHugh

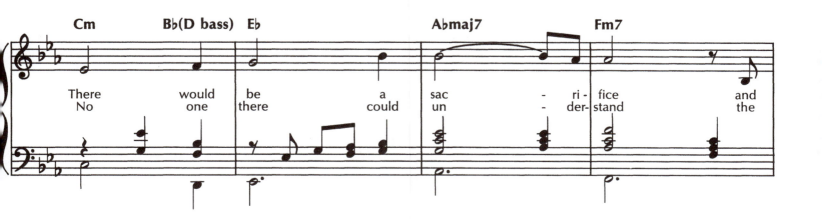

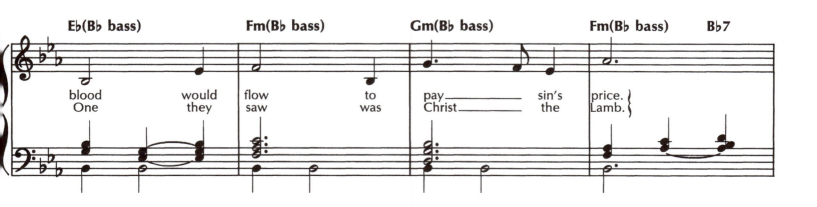

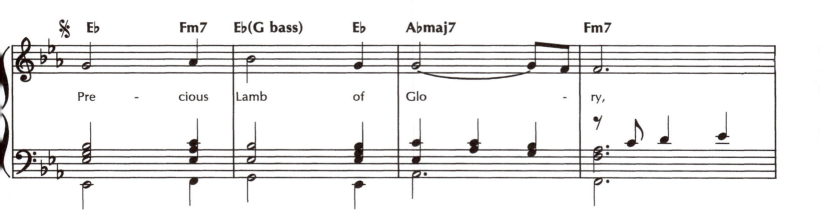

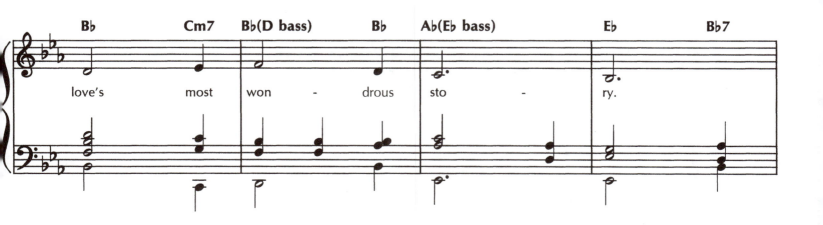

# O Master, Let Me Walk with Thee

**Electronic and Pipe Organs**
Upper: Clar. 8', Fls. 8', 4'
Lower: Horn 8' (Fl.), Stgs. 8', 4'
Pedal: Soft 16' to Gt.

**Drawbar Organs**
Upper: 00 6725 400 (00)
Lower: (00) 4454 321 (0)
Pedal: 4 (0) 2 (0) (Spinet 3)

Words by Washington Gladden
Music by H. Percy Smith

# Via Dolorosa

Electronic Organs
Upper: Strings 8', 4', Clarinet
Lower: Diapason 8', Flute 8'
Pedals: String Bass
Vib./Trem.: On, Slow

Drawbar Organs
Upper: 55 6606 001
Lower: 00 6543 001
Pedals: 46
Vib./Trem.: On, Slow

Words and Music by Billy Sprague
and Niles Borop

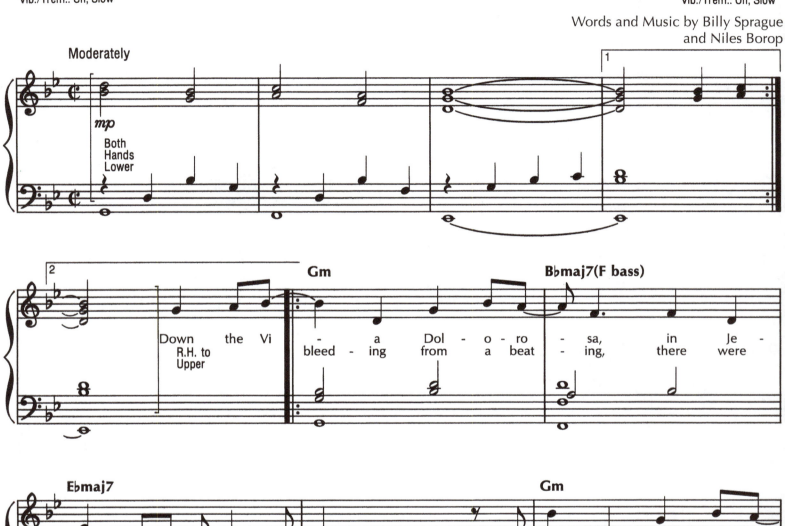

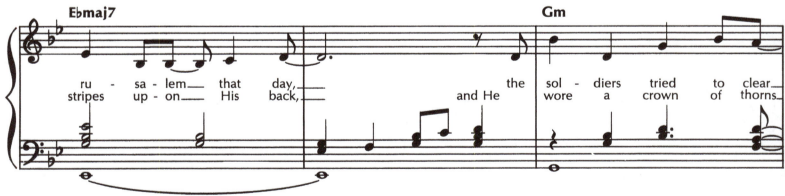

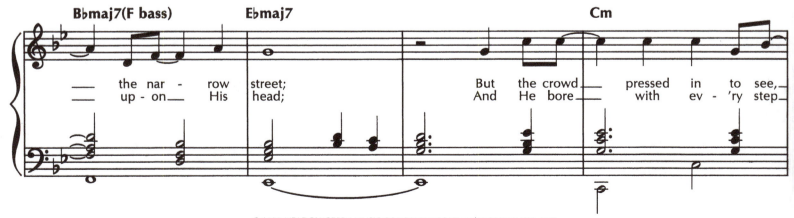

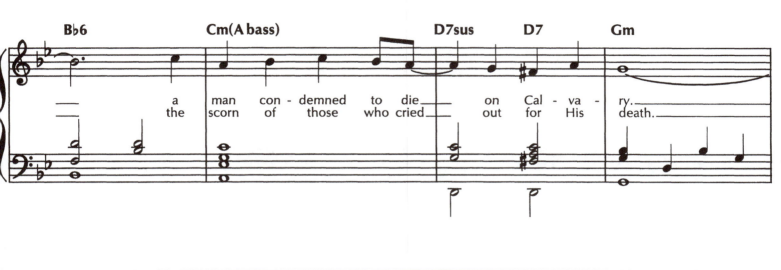

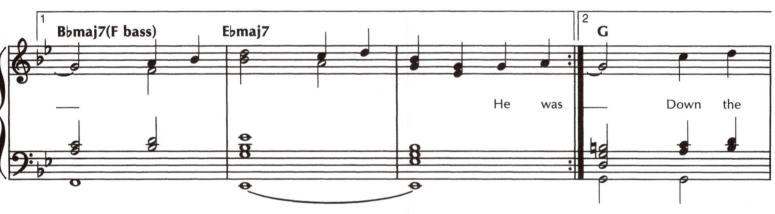

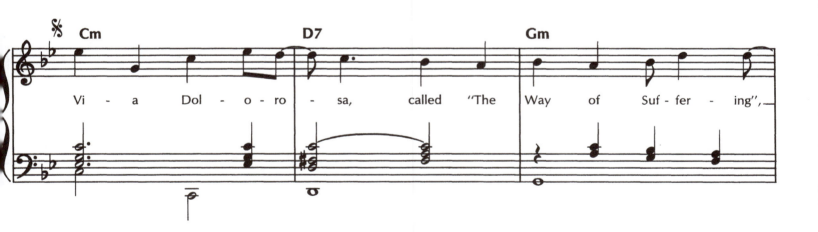

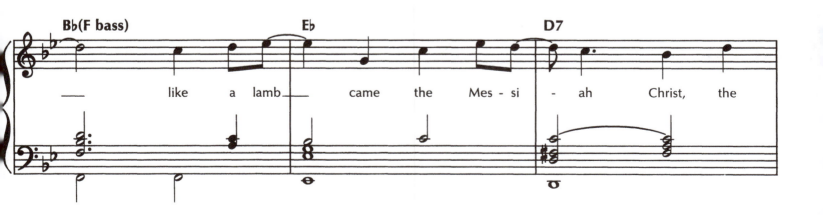

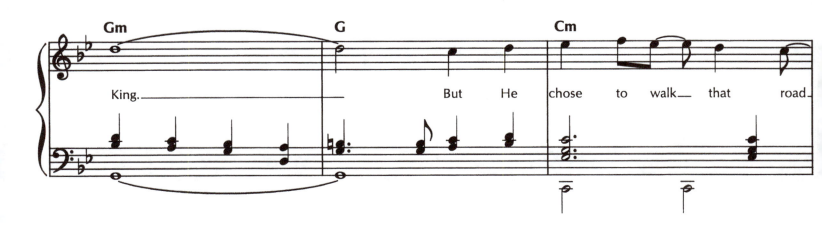

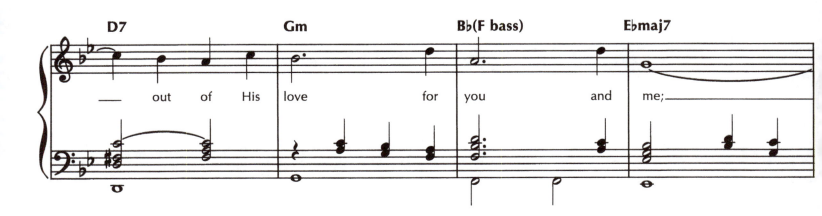

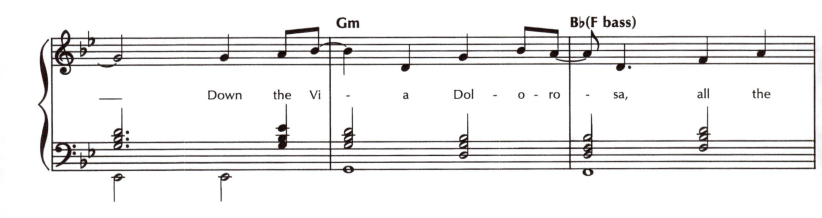

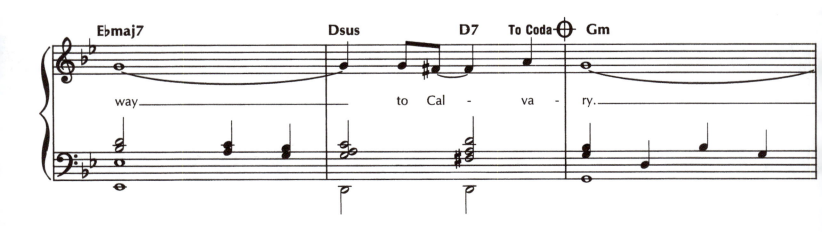

31

# Were You There?

Electronic and Pipe Organs

Upper: Soft 8′ Stgs.
Lower: Fr. Horn (Solo Fl.) 8′
Pedal: Soft 16′

Drawbar Organs

Upper: 00 4432 210 (00)
Lower: (00) 7650 000 (0)
Pedal: 3 (0) 1 (0) (Spinet 2)

Traditional Spiritual

# El Shaddai

Electronic Organs
Upper: Flutes (or Tibias) 8', 4'
        Oboe
Lower: Melodia 8', String 4'
Pedal: 16', 8'
Vib./Trem: On, Fast

Drawbar Organs
Upper: 24 6604 010
Lower: (00) 7732 210
Pedal: 43
Vib./Trem: On, Fast

Words and Music by Michael Card
and John Thompson

With much expression

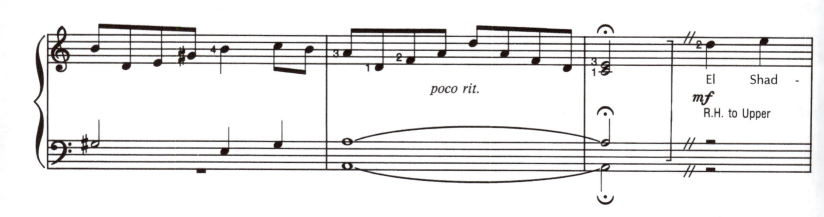

36

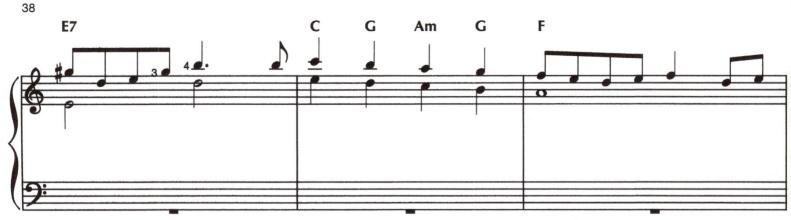

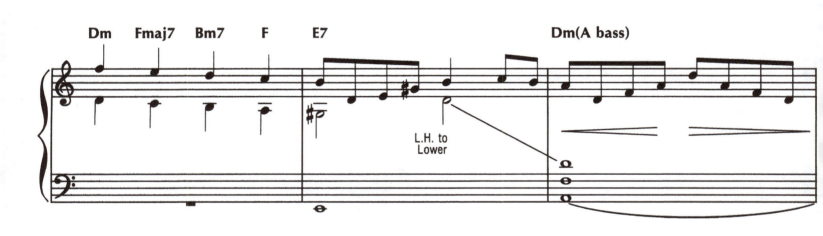

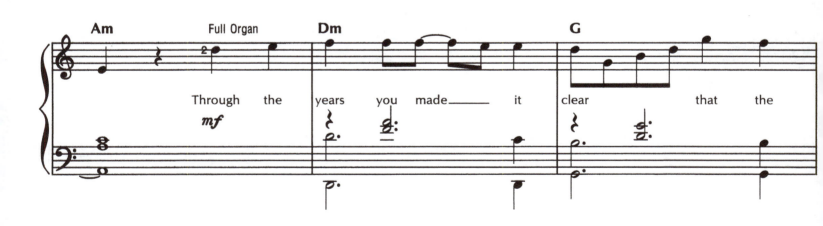

Through the years you made it clear that the

time of Christ was near, though the peo - ple could - n't

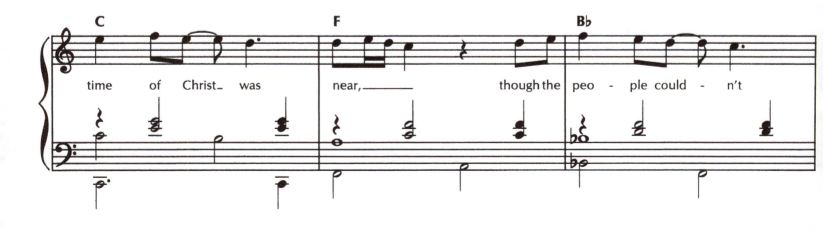

39

# God So Loved the World

**ALL ELECTRONIC ORGANS**
**Upper:** Flute 16'(Bourdon 16')
Flute 8'
**Lower:** Diapason 8', Melodia 8'
**Pedal:** 16', 8' Medium
**Vibrato:** Off

**ALL DRAWBAR ORGANS**
**Upper:** 00 8740 000
**Lower:** (00) 4433 222 (2)
**Pedal:** 4-2 (Spinet 2)
**Vibrato:** Off

Words from John 3:16, 17
Music by John Stainer

Slowly and solemnly

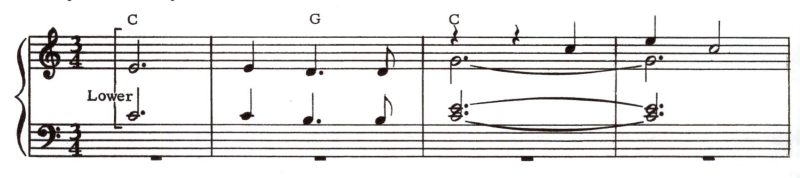

41

# Jesus, Lord to Me

Electronic Organs
Upper: Clarinet, Flutes 8', 4'
Lower: Diapason 8', Tibias 8', 4'
Pedals: 16', 8'
Vib./Trem.: On, Fast

Drawbar Organs
Upper: 00 8271 610
Lower: 00 5544 210
Pedals: 64
Vib./Trem.: On, Fast

Words and Music by Greg Nelson
and Gary McSpadden

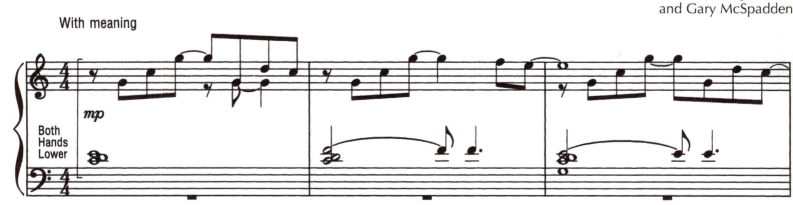

With meaning

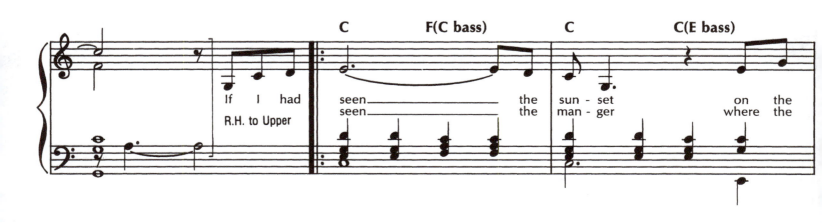

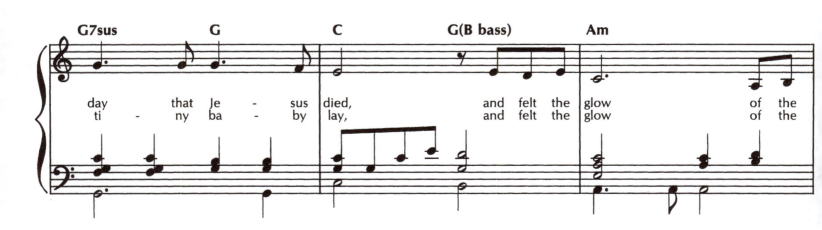

45

46

# Jesus, the Very Thought of Thee

Electronic and Pipe Organs

Upper: Clar. 8', Fl. 16', 8'
Lower: Stg. 8' and Soft 4'
Pedal: Soft 16' to Gt.

Drawbar Organs

Upper: 65 5725 000 (00)
Lower: (00) 4454 321 (0)
Pedal: 4 (0) 2 (0) (Spinet 3)

Words attributed to Bernard of Clairvaux
Music by John Bacchus Dykes

* May be played an octave lower 2nd time ad. lib. with 16' off.

49

# Lamb of God

**Electronic Organs**
Upper: Flutes (or Tibias) 16', 8', 4'
Lower: Strings 8', Diapason
Pedal: String Bass
Vib./Trem: On, Fast

**Drawbar Organs**
Upper: 80 4800 000
Lower: (00) 7334 01
Pedal: String Bass
Vib./Trem: On, Fast

Words and Music by
Twila Paris

# Thy Word

Electronic Organs
Upper: Flutes 16',8',4', Oboe
Lower: Flutes 8',4', String 8'
Pedals: String Bass
Vib./Trem.: On, Slow

Drawbar Organs
Upper: 60 0608 001
Lower: 00 6345 211
Pedals: 45
Vib./Trem.: On, Slow

Words and Music by Michael W. Smith
and Amy Grant

54

# People Need the Lord

Electronic Organs
Upper: Flutes (or Tibias) 8', 4'
      Clarinet
Lower: Melodia 8', Reed 8'
Pedal: 8'
Vib./Trem: On, Fast

Drawbar Organs
Upper: 83 0314 013
Lower: (00) 7401 001
Pedal: 24
Vib./Trem: On, Fast

Words and Music by Phill McHugh
and Greg Nelson

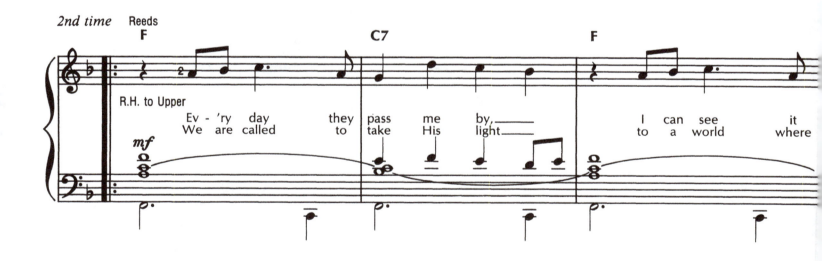

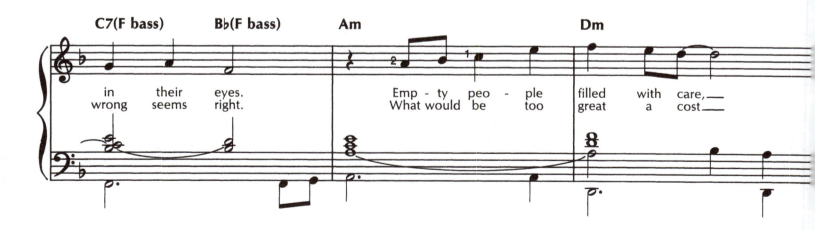

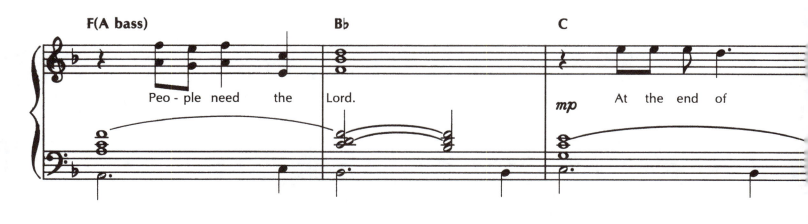

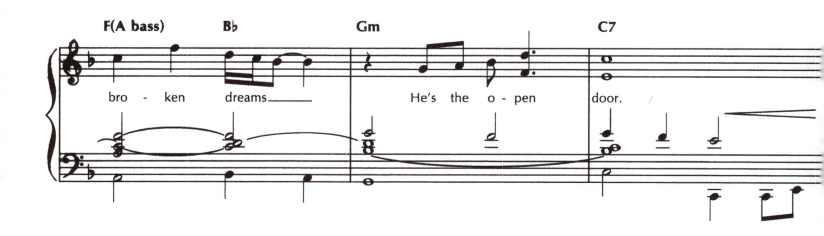

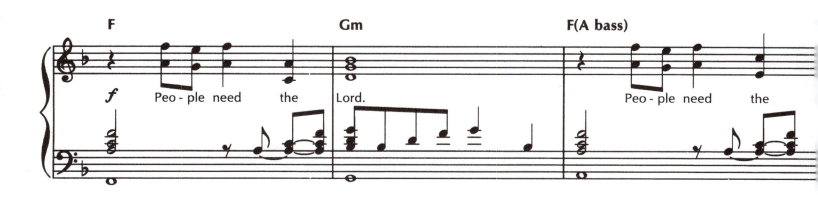

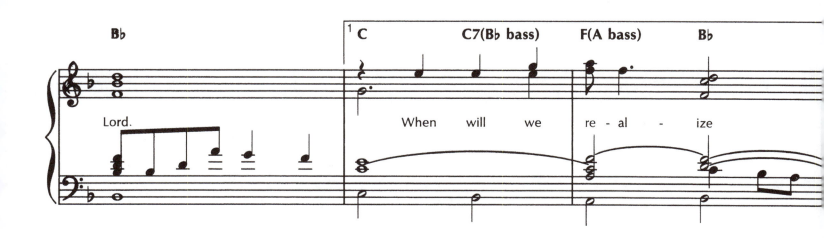

# Rock of Ages

**Electronic and Pipe Organs**
Upper:   Fr. Horn (Fl.) 8'
Lower:   Stgs. 8', 4'
Pedal:   Soft 16' to Gt.

**Drawbar Organs**
Upper:   00 8850 000 (00)
Lower:   (00) 6116 432 (0)
Pedal:   4 (0) 2 (0)   (Spinet 3)

Words by Augustus M. Toplady
Music by Thomas Hastings

# Sweet Hour of Prayer

Electronic and Pipe Organs .

Upper:   Fr. Horn (Fl.) 8'
Lower:   Stgs. 8', 4'
Pedal:   Soft 16' to Gt.

Drawbar Organs

Upper:   00  8850 000 (00)
Lower:   (00) 6116 432 (0)
Pedal:   4 (0) 2 (0)  (Spinet 3'

Words by William W. Walford
Music by William B. Bradbury

# What a Friend We Have in Jesus

**Electronic and Pipe Organs**

Upper: Fr. Horn (Solo Fl.) 8'
Lower: Stgs. 8', 4'
Pedal: Soft 16' to Gt.

**Drawbar Organs**

Upper: 00 8585 000 (00)
Lower: (00) 5545 321 (0)
Pedal: 4 (0) 2 (0) (Spinet 3

Words by Joseph M. Scriven
Music by Charles C. Converse

*Andante devoto - calmato (M.M. ♩ = 52)*

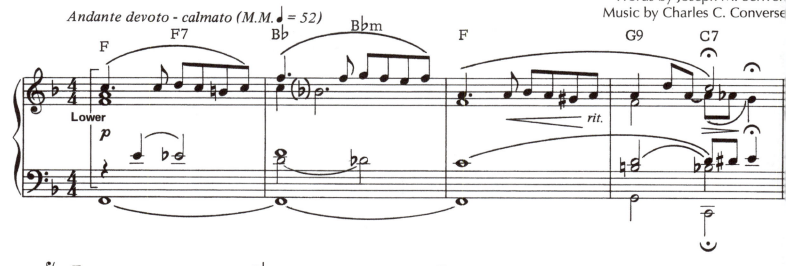

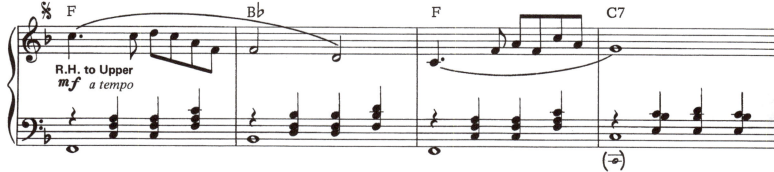

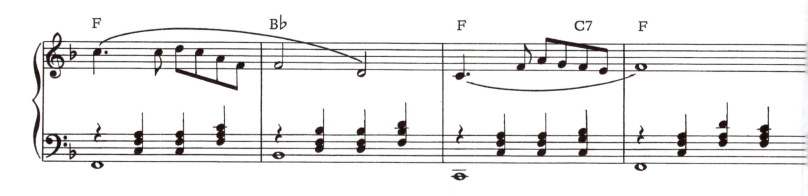

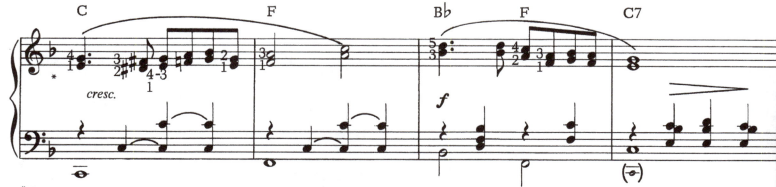

\* Play top notes only if desired.

2nd time only ad lib.
8va
2nd time to Coda
F
F7
Bb
F
C7
F
mf
dim. e rit.
Piu mosso (in 2) (M.M. 𝅗𝅥 = 63)
Bb
C#dim
F7
Bb
Eb
Lower
mf
No Pedal
Bb
C7
F
F+
Bb
Bb7
C#dim Ebm6
Bb
C7
(b5)
Bb
Eb
F7
Bb
rit.
p
(R.H. to Upper)
D.S. al Coda
Coda
Dm
F
F7
Bb
F
C
F
(loco)
Lower
p
rit.

# Battle Hymn of the Republic

**Electronic and Pipe Organs**

Upper: *ff*, no heavy reeds
Lower: *ff*, with solo reeds
Pedal: *ff* to Sw.

**Drawbar Organs**

Upper: 40 6678 452 (00)
Lower: (00) 8876 543 (0)
Pedal: 7 (0) 5 (0) (Spinet 6)

Words by Julia Ward Howe
Music by William Steffe

*Detached, **not** staccato

# The Glory of God in Nature

**ALL ELECTRONIC ORGANS**
Upper: Flute 8', 4', Oboe 8'
     (Reed 8')
Lower: Diapason 8'
Pedal: 16', 8' Medium

**ALL DRAWBAR ORGANS**
Upper:   63 7748 336
Lower:  (00) 6536 334 (1)
Pedal:    4-2 (Spinet 3)

By Ludwig van Beethoven

**Slowly and majestically**

# Great Is the Lord

Electronic Organs
Upper: Strings 8', 4'
Lower: Reed 8'
Pedal: 16'
Vib./Trem: On, Slow

Drawbar Organs
Upper: 63 5325 004
Lower: (00) 6324 312
Pedal: 44
Vib./Trem: On, Slow

Words and Music by Michael W. Smith
and Deborah D. Smith

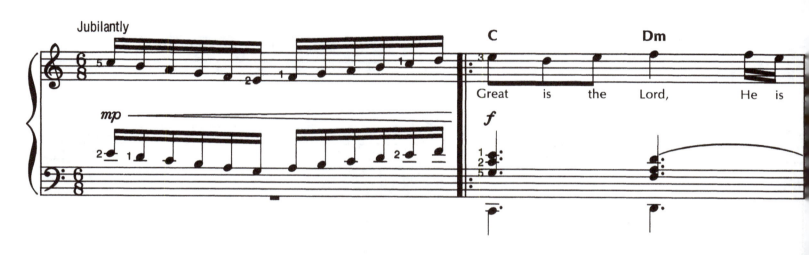

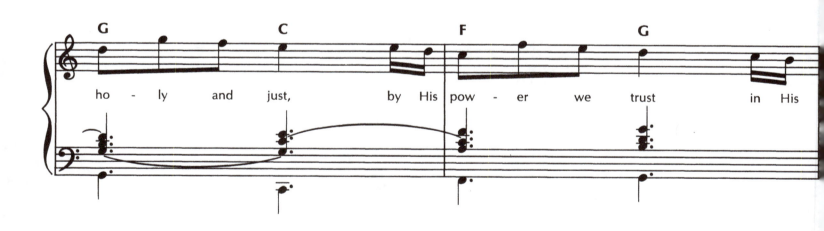

# He Is Exalted

**Electronic Organs**
Upper: Full Brass (Trumpets, Trombones)
Lower: Strings 8', 4'
Pedal: 16', 8'
Vib./Trem.: On, Slow

**Drawbar Organs**
Upper: 80 7766 008
Lower: (00) 8076 000
Pedal: 34
Vib./Trem.: On, Slow

Words and Music by
Twila Paris

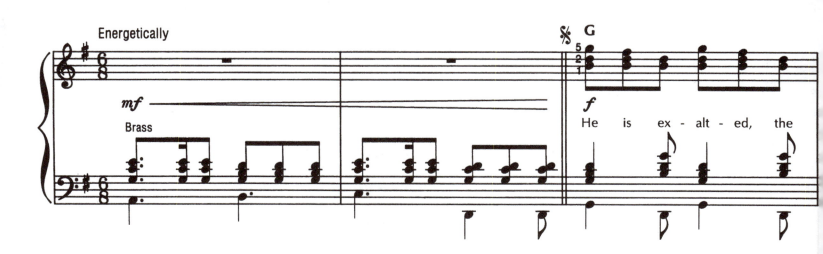

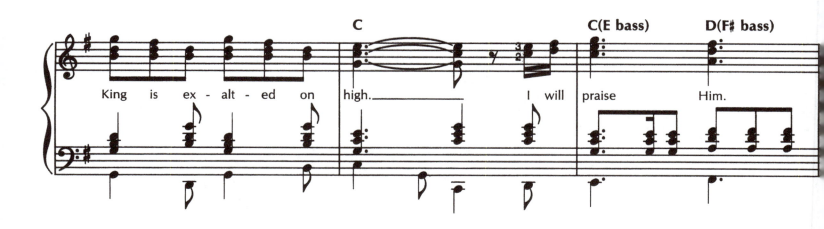

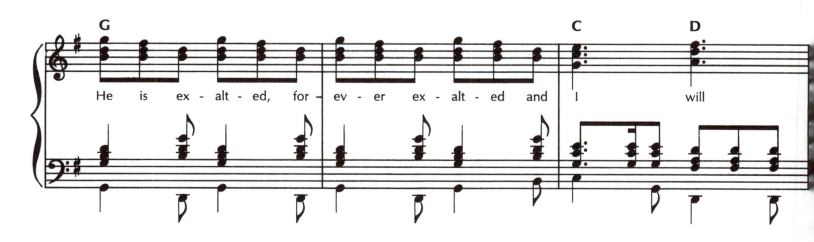

# Hosanna, Loud Hosanna
## (with "All Glory, Laud and Honor")

**ALL ELECTRONIC ORGANS**
Upper:  Trumpet 8', Saxophone 8'
        (Reed 8'), Horn 8'
Lower:  Violin 8' (String 8'), Horn 8'
Pedal:  16', 8' Medium
Vibrato: Off

**ALL DRAWBAR ORGANS**
Upper:  40 6847 336
Lower:  (00) 6634 224 (2)
Pedal:  5-3 (Spinet 4)
Vibrato: Off

Words by Jenette Threlfall, based on Matthew 21:1–11
Music taken from *Gesangbuch der Herzogl*

## All Glory, Laud and Honor

# Lead On, O King Eternal

**ALL ELECTRONIC ORGANS**
Upper:   Flute 8', 4', Oboe 8'
            (Reed 8')
Lower:   Diapason 8'
Pedal:   16', 8' Medium
Vibrato: Off

**ALL DRAWBAR ORGANS**
Upper:   40 7858 347
Lower:   (00) 6764 554 (0)
Pedal:   5-4 (Spinet 4)
Vibrato: Off

Words by Ernest W. Shurtleff
Music by Henry T. Smart

Brightly - With  Majesty

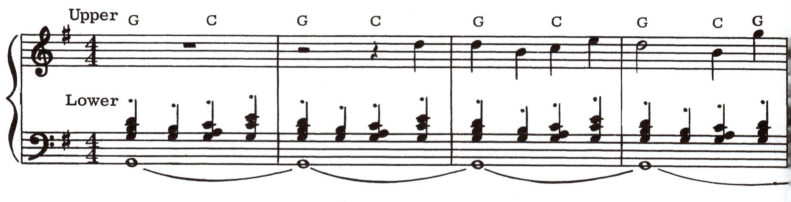

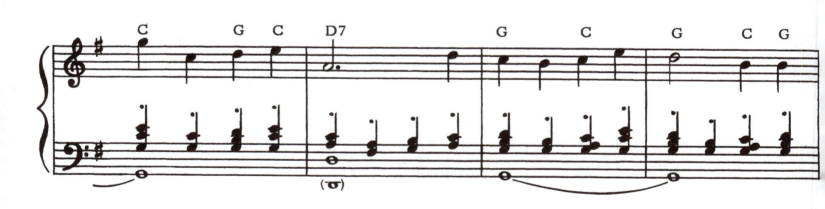

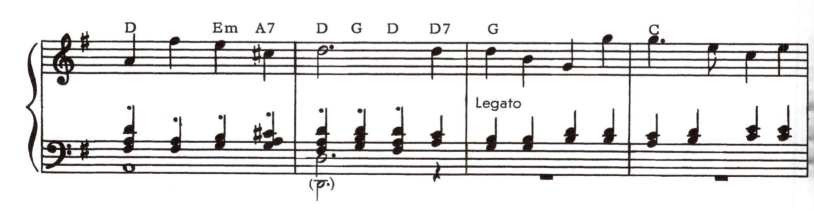

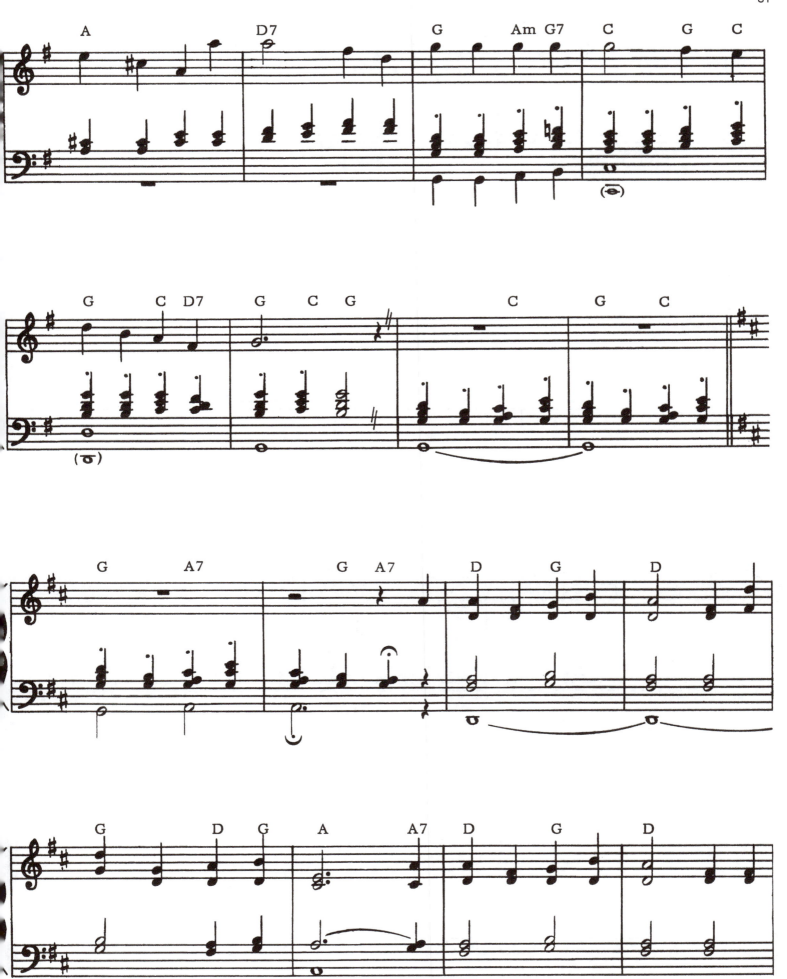

82

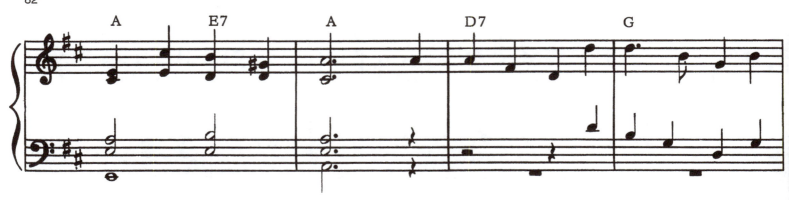

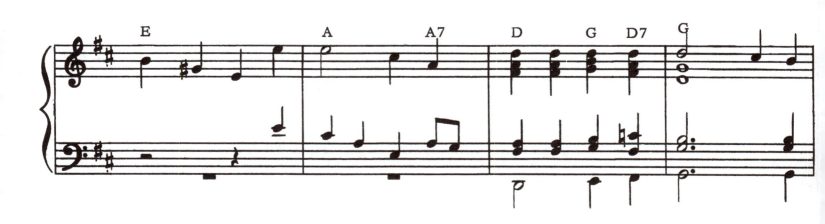

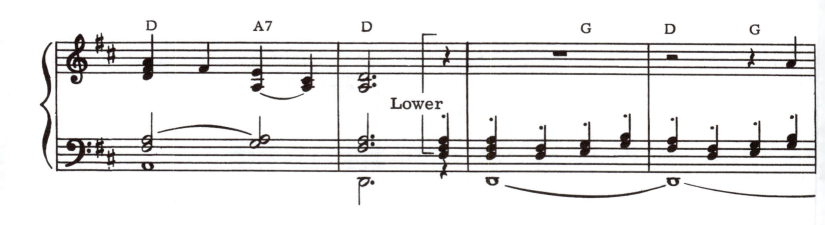

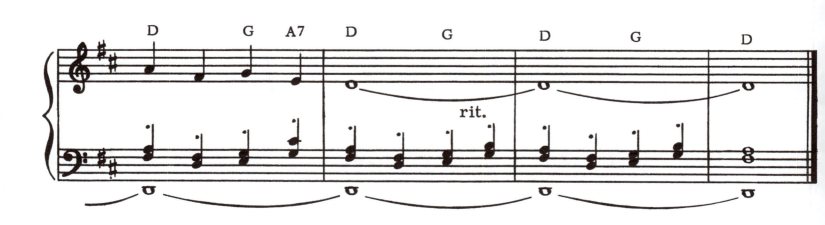

# O Magnify the Lord

Electronic Organs
Upper: Flutes 16', 8', 4', 2'
Strings 8', 4'
Lower: Flutes 8', 4', String 8'
Pedals: 16', 8'
Vib./Trem.: Off

Drawbar Organs
Upper: 80 7104 001
Lower: 00 8512 002
Pedals: 65
Vib./Trem.: Off

Words and Music by Melodie Tunney
and Dick Tunney

# A Mighty Fortress Is Our God

**Electronic and Pipe Organs**

Upper: Full, with 16' and soft reed(s)
Lower: Full, with 16' and soft reed(s) (all couplers)
Pedal: *ff* 16' and 8' with Op. Diapason(s) and soft
reed(s) (all couplers)

**Drawbar Organs**

Upper: 56 8888 765 (54)
Lower: (44) 8888 7655 (5)
Pedal: 8 (0) 6 (0) (Spinet 8)

Words and Music by Martin Luther
Based on Psalm 46

*Set stops and drawbars at "full organ" for ending phrase.

# Proclaim the Glory of the Lord

Electronic Organs
Upper: Flutes (or Tibias) 16′, 4′
  Trumpet, Trombone
Lower: Flute 8′, Diapason 8′
  (opt. String 4′)
Pedal: 16′, 8′
Vib./Trem: On, Slow

Drawbar Organs
Upper: 82 5864 210
Lower: (00) 7103 000
Pedal: 44
Vib./Trem: On, Slow

Words and Music by Dwight Liles
and Niles Borop

# O Worship the King

ALL ELECTRONIC ORGANS
Upper:  Cello 16', Trumpet 8',
        Flute 8', 4'
Lower:  Reed 8', Viola 8' (String 8')
Pedal:  16', 8' Full
Vibrato: Off

ALL DRAWBAR ORGANS
Upper:  52 7866 354
Lower:  (00) 5624 334 (2)
Pedal:  6-2 (Spinet 3)
Vibrato: Off

Words by Robert Grant
Music by William Croft

G D7 Em D G D A7 D
Em Em7 C Bm
Lower
f
C G D7 G C Am D7 G
rit.
Lower mf
D7 G D C
D7 G C D G
p
rit.

# The Best Sacred Collections for Piano

## Blended Worship Piano Collection

Songs include: Amazing Grace (My Chains Are Gone) • Be Thou My Vision • I Will Rise • Joyful, Joyful, We Adore Thee • Lamb of God • Majesty • Open the Eyes of My Heart • Praise to the Lord, the Almighty • Shout to the Lord • 10,000 Reasons (Bless the Lord) • Worthy Is the Lamb • Your Name • and more.
00293528 Piano Solo ...............................$17.99

## Hymn Anthology

A beautiful collection of 60 hymns arranged for piano solo, including: Abide with Me • Be Thou My Vision • Come, Thou Fount of Every Blessing • Doxology • For the Beauty of the Earth • God of Grace and God of Glory • Holy, Holy, Holy • It Is Well with My Soul • Joyful, Joyful, We Adore Thee • Let Us Break Bread Together • A Mighty Fortress Is Our God • O God, Our Help in Ages Past • Savior, like a Shepherd Lead Us • To God Be the Glory • What a Friend We Have in Jesus • and more.
00251244 Piano Solo .............................$16.99

## The Hymn Collection

*arranged by Phillip Keveren*

17 beloved hymns expertly and beautifully arranged for solo piano by Phillip Keveren. Includes: All Hail the Power of Jesus' Name • I Love to Tell the Story • I Surrender All • I've Got Peace Like a River • Were You There? • and more.
00311071 Piano Solo .............................$14.99

## Hymn Duets

*arranged by Phillip Keveren*

Includes lovely duet arrangements of: All Creatures of Our God and King • I Surrender All • It Is Well with My Soul • O Sacred Head, Now Wounded • Praise to the Lord, The Almighty • Rejoice, The Lord Is King • and more.
00311544 Piano Duet.............................$14.99

## Hymn Medleys

*arranged by Phillip Keveren*

Great medleys resonate with the human spirit, as do the truths in these moving hymns. Here Phillip Keveren combines 24 timeless favorites into eight lovely medleys for solo piano.
00311349 Piano Solo .............................$14.99

## Hymns for Two

*arranged by Carol Klose*

12 piano duet arrangements of favorite hymns: Amazing Grace • Be Thou My Vision • Crown Him with Many Crowns • Fairest Lord Jesus • Holy, Holy, Holy • I Need Thee Every Hour • O Worship the King • What a Friend We Have in Jesus • and more.
00290544 Piano Duet.............................$12.99

## It Is Well
### 10 BELOVED HYMNS FOR MEMORIAL SERVICES

*arr. John Purifoy*

10 peaceful, soul-stirring hymn settings appropriate for memorial services and general worship use. Titles include: Abide with Me • Amazing Grace • Be Still My Soul • For All the Saints • His Eye Is on the Sparrow • In the Garden • It Is Well with My Soul • Like a River Glorious • Rock of Ages • What a Friend We Have in Jesus.
00118920 Piano Solo .............................$12.99

## Ragtime Gospel Classics

*arr. Steven K. Tedesco*

A dozen old-time gospel favorites: Because He Lives • Goodbye World Goodbye • He Touched Me • I Saw the Light • I'll Fly Away • Keep on the Firing Line • Mansion over the Hilltop • No One Ever Cared for Me like Jesus • There Will Be Peace in the Valley for Me • Victory in Jesus • What a Day That Will Be • Where Could I Go.
00142449 Piano Solo .............................$11.99

## Ragtime Gospel Hymns

*arranged by Steven Tedesco*

15 traditional gospel hymns, including: At Calvary • Footsteps of Jesus • Just a Closer Walk with Thee • Leaning on the Everlasting Arms • What a Friend We Have in Jesus • When We All Get to Heaven • and more.
00311763 Piano Solo .............................$10.99

## Sacred Classics for Solo Piano

*arr. John Purifoy*

10 timeless songs of faith, masterfully arranged by John Purifoy. Because He Lives • Easter Song • Glorify Thy Name • Here Am I, Send Me • I'd Rather Have Jesus • Majesty • On Eagle's Wings • There's Something About That Name • We Shall Behold Him • Worthy Is the Lamb.
00141703 Piano Solo .............................$14.99

## Raise Your Hands
### PIANO SOLOS FOR BLENDED WORSHIP

*arr. Heather Sorenson*

10 uplifting and worshipful solos crafted by Heather Sorenson. Come Thou Fount, Come Thou King • God of Heaven • Holy Is the Lord (with "Holy, Holy, Holy") • Holy Spirit • I Will Rise • In Christ Alone • Raise Your Hands • Revelation Song • 10,000 Reasons (Bless the Lord) • Your Name (with "All Hail the Power of Jesus' Name").
00231579 Piano Solo .............................$14.99

## Seasonal Sunday Solos for Piano

24 blended selections grouped by occasion. Includes: Breath of Heaven (Mary's Song) • Come, Ye Thankful People, Come • Do You Hear What I Hear • God of Our Fathers • In the Name of the Lord • Mary, Did You Know? • Mighty to Save • Spirit of the Living God • The Wonderful Cross • and more.
00311971 Piano Solo .............................$16.99

## Sunday Solos for Piano

30 blended selections, perfect for the church pianist. Songs include: All Hail the Power of Jesus' Name • Be Thou My Vision • Great Is the Lord • Here I Am to Worship • Majesty • Open the Eyes of My Heart • and many more.
00311272 Piano Solo .............................$17.99

## More Sunday Solos for Piano

A follow-up to *Sunday Solos for Piano*, this collection features 30 more blended selections perfect for the church pianist. Includes: Agnus Dei • Come, Thou Fount of Every Blessing • The Heart of Worship • How Great Thou Art • Immortal, Invisible • O Worship the King • Shout to the Lord • Thy Word • We Fall Down • and more.
00311864 Piano Solo .............................$16.99

## Even More Sunday Solos for Piano

30 blended selections, including: Ancient Words • Brethren, We Have Met to Worship • How Great Is Our God • Lead On, O King Eternal • Offering • Savior, Like a Shepherd Lead Us • We Bow Down • Worthy of Worship • and more.
00312098 Piano Solo .............................$16.99

P/V/G = Piano/Vocal/Guitar arrangements.

Prices, contents and availability subject to change without notice.

0122
001

# The Best
# PRAISE & WORSHIP
## Songbooks for Piano

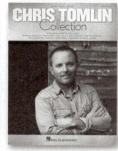

### Above All
THE PHILLIP KEVEREN SERIES
15 beautiful praise song piano solo arrangements by Phillip Keveren. Includes: Above All • Agnus Dei • Breathe • Draw Me Close • He Is Exalted • I Stand in Awe • Step by Step • We Fall Down • You Are My King (Amazing Love) • and more.
00311024 Piano Solo .................................. $12.99

### Blended Worship Piano Collection
Songs include: Amazing Grace (My Chains Are Gone) • Be Thou My Vision • Cornerstone • Fairest Lord Jesus • Great Is Thy Faithfulness • How Great Is Our God • I Will Rise • Joyful, Joyful, We Adore Thee • Lamb of God • Majesty • Open the Eyes of My Heart • Praise to the Lord, the Almighty • Shout to the Lord • 10,000 Reasons (Bless the Lord) • Worthy Is the Lamb • Your Name • and more.
00293528 Piano Solo ..................................$17.99

### Blessings
THE PHILLIP KEVEREN SERIES
Phillip Keveren delivers another stellar collection of piano solo arrangements perfect for any reverent or worship setting: Blessed Be Your Name • Blessings • Cornerstone • Holy Spirit • This Is Amazing Grace • We Believe • Your Great Name • Your Name • and more.
00156601 Piano Solo ................................ $12.99

### The Best Praise & Worship Songs Ever
80 all-time favorites: Awesome God • Breathe • Days of Elijah • Here I Am to Worship • I Could Sing of Your Love Forever • Open the Eyes of My Heart • Shout to the Lord • We Bow Down • dozens more.
00311057 P/V/G.................................... $22.99

### The Big Book of Praise & Worship
Over 50 worship favorites are presented in this popular "Big Book" series collection. Includes: Always • Cornerstone • Forever Reign • I Will Follow • Jesus Paid It All • Lord, I Need You • Mighty to Save • Our God • Stronger • 10,000 Reasons (Bless the Lord) • This Is Amazing Grace • and more.
00140795 P/V/G ......................................... $24.99

### Contemporary Worship Duets
*arr. Bill Wolaver*
Contains 8 powerful songs carefully arranged by Bill Wolaver as duets for intermediate-level players: Agnus Dei • Be unto Your Name • He Is Exalted • Here I Am to Worship • I Will Rise • The Potter's Hand • Revelation Song • Your Name.
00290593 Piano Duets ............................. $10.99

### The Best of Passion
Over 40 worship favorites featuring the talents of David Crowder, Matt Redman, Chris Tomlin, and others. Songs include: Always • Awakening • Blessed Be Your Name • Jesus Paid It All • My Heart Is Yours • Our God • 10,000 Reasons (Bless the Lord) • and more.
00101888 P/V/G .................................... $19.99

### Praise & Worship Duets
THE PHILLIP KEVEREN SERIES
8 worshipful duets by Phillip Keveren: As the Deer • Awesome God • Give Thanks • Great Is the Lord • Lord, I Lift Your Name on High • Shout to the Lord • There Is a Redeemer • We Fall Down.
00311203 Piano Duet................................. $12.99

### Shout to the Lord!
THE PHILLIP KEVEREN SERIES
14 favorite praise songs, including: As the Deer • El Shaddai • Give Thanks • Great Is the Lord • How Beautiful • More Precious Than Silver • Oh Lord, You're Beautiful • A Shield About Me • Shine, Jesus, Shine • Shout to the Lord • Thy Word • and more.
00310699 Piano Solo ............................... $14.99

### Sunday Solos in the Key of C
CLASSIC & CONTEMPORARY WORSHIP SONGS
22 C-major selections, including: Above All • Good Good Father • His Name Is Wonderful • Holy Spirit • Lord, I Need You • Reckless Love • What a Beautiful Name • You Are My All in All • and more.
00301044 Piano Solo ............................... $14.99

### The Chris Tomlin Collection – 2nd Edition
15 songs from one of the leading artists and composers in Contemporary Christian music, including the favorites: Amazing Grace (My Chains Are Gone) • Holy Is the Lord • How Can I Keep from Singing • How Great Is Our God • Jesus Messiah • Our God • We Fall Down • and more.
00306951 P/V/G .............................. $17.99

### Top Christian Downloads
21 of Christian music's top hits are presented in this collection of intermediate level piano solo arrangements. Includes: Forever Reign • How Great Is Our God • Mighty to Save • Praise You in This Storm • 10,000 Reasons (Bless the Lord) • Your Grace Is Enough • and more.
00125051 Piano Solo................................. $14.99

### Top 25 Worship Songs
25 contemporary worship hits includes: Glorious Day (Passion) • Good, Good Father (Chris Tomlin) • Holy Spirit (Francesca Battistelli) • King of My Heart (John Mark & Sarah McMillan) • The Lion and the Lamb (Big Daddy Weave) • Reckless Love (Cory Asbury) • 10,000 Reasons (Matt Redman) • This Is Amazing Grace (Phil Wickham) • What a Beautiful Name (Hillsong Worship) • and more.
00288610 P/V/G ..............................$17.99

### Top Worship Downloads
20 of today's chart-topping Christian hits, including: Cornerstone • Forever Reign • Great I Am • Here for You • Lord, I Need You • My God • Never Once • One Thing Remains (Your Love Never Fails) • Your Great Name • and more.
00120870 P/V/G ...................................... $16.99

### The World's Greatest Praise Songs
*Shawnee Press*
This is a unique and useful collection of 50 of the very best praise titles of the last three decades. Includes: Above All • Forever • Here I Am to Worship • I Could Sing of Your Love Forever • Open the Eyes of My Heart • and so many more.
35022891 P/V/G ......................................... $19.99

## HAL•LEONARD®
### www.halleonard.com
P/V/G = Piano/Vocal/Guitar Arrangements
Prices, contents, and availability subject to change without notice.